J. N Söderholm

The Silver Question

J. N Söderholm

The Silver Question

ISBN/EAN: 9783743320628

Manufactured in Europe, USA, Canada, Australia, Japa

Cover: Foto ©ninafisch / pixelio.de

Manufactured and distributed by brebook publishing software
(www.brebook.com)

J. N Söderholm

The Silver Question

SILVER QUESTION

— BY —

J. N. SÖDERHOLM.

CHICAGO:
THE REGAN PRINTING HOUSE,
1896.

CONTENTS.

Page.

Preface 5

Introduction 9

Money 16

Retail Transactions 21

Wholesale Transactions 25

Cost of Production and Prices 29

Cost of Production of Gold and Silver 32

Do We Need More Money? 41

Bi-Metallism 51

What Would Happen if We Adopt the Ratio of of 16 to 1? 58

Conclusion 66

PREFACE.

A quarter of a century of discussion and agitation seems to have brought about an appreciable change in the sentiment of the people on the silver question, all over the world, and particularly in this country. The insufficiency of the supply of gold and the evil of falling prices consequent upon the constant discriminations against silver, have at last stirred the public, who now look for a remedy in the remonetization of the white metal.

We have in this country practically three monetary parties, to wit:

1. Those who want the unlimited coinage of silver and gold at the ratio of 16 to 1.
2. Those who want our metallic money to consist of gold and silver of full value, or who want true bimetallism.
3. Those who want the gold standard.

What would be the consequence of the adoption of unlimited coinage at 16 to 1 can be reasonably calculated. How and to what extent the bimetallists could add full value silver money to our circulation without disturbing the gold is a question upon the satisfactory solution of which depends the conciliation of the gold standard party as well as of the ardent friends of silver.

If this country alone is to undertake, or to start, the restoration of bimetallism, or of silver, it must adopt a policy which would satisfy the following conditions:

1. Not to disturb materially our present monetary system.
2. Not to add to our coinage such a quantity of silver as to drive out any of our gold.
3. To make the silver money good the world over.
4. To make the new silver dollar of same size as the old silver dollar.
5. To make the coinage unlimited.

6. To coin silver from any part of the world.
7. To fix the price of silver—barring the exchanges—for the whole world.
8. To cause the government no loss except the cost of coining.

If a measure fulfilling all the above mentioned conditions can be framed, I think it would follow:

1. That our present gold monometallists would offer no objection to the adoption of bimetallism.
2. That in the course of a very short time the truth of the principles of bimetallism would again have been practically demonstrated.
3. That in the near future other countries, one after another, would hasten to adopt bimetallism, which would soon become general or universal.
4. That, within a few years, possibly before the close of this century, bimetallism, with free and unlimited coinage of

silver and gold at the old ratio of 15 1-2 to 1, or 16 to 1, would be firmly established.

Such a measure can be framed. I am satisfied that the adoption of unlimited coinage of silver and gold at the ratio of 16 to 1 would fill the bill. But in adopting unlimited coinage we might placate opponents by gradually increasing the gold in reserve for the greenbacks and by charging, until further, on the coinage of silver a seigniorage which would tend to limit the production of the white metal.

INTRODUCTION.

The silver question of to-day is not the silver question of five years ago, nor was the silver question of five years ago the silver question of twenty years ago. The downfall of silver has been gradual, one nation after another discontinuing the coinage of the white metal for the purpose of unlimited legal tender money, until at present it would seem as if we had reached the bottom, and as if—providing silver is to be rehabilitated—the time had now come for rehabilitation, or at least for the beginning of an upward movement which in the course of a short time would culminate in the complete restoration of silver, the re-establishment of bimetallism at the ratio of 15 1-2 to 1, or 16 to 1.

If, when Germany had adopted the single gold standard, she had not been in such a hurry to accumulate gold and dispose of her silver, I think bimetallism would not have been seriously endangered. But while France had to pay the war indemnity, and Germany flooded the market with silver, which more or less directly found its way to the French mint, the capacity of the latter was so overtaxed that before the closing of the same there was in stock for coinage so much silver bullion that it would take a year to coin it. The bullion certificates issued by the mint could be discounted, but, naturally, the value of silver bullion was reduced by the discount on the certificates. If the change of standard in Germany had extended over a period of ten or fifteen years the price of silver would not have fallen several per cent, France would easily have been able to bear the burden of the German innovation, financiers of other countries would not have been frightened, bimetallism would have been preserved, and the whole world would have been benefited.

But the principles of bimetallism were not understood. The statesmen of the time had imbibed their wisdom from the teachings of John Stuart Mill: a double standard was a physical impossibility. And so one country after another closed its mints against further coinage of silver, and for every new demonetization the difficulties for the balance of the world to restore the old order of things became greater. Yet even in 1879, on the resumption of specie payments, this country would in all probability have been powerful enough to re-establish bimetallism by adopting unlimited coinage of silver and gold at the ratio of 16 to 1. Such action would unquestionably have restored, at that time, the value of silver. It would most probably have brought back the Latin Union to its old policy, stopped further demonetizations, encouraged other countries about to resume specie payments to adopt the double standard, and thus solved the whole question. The Bland-Allison bill might possibly have brought about a similar result if the secretary of the treasury had not discriminated against the maximum coinage of $4,000,000 of silver a month, for at that time such maximum coinage would probably have been equivalent in effect to the adoption of unlimited coinage. As the Bland act was administered, however, it certainly fell short of supplying the requisite remedy to restore bimetallism. When, later, the Sherman act was passed, the appreciation of gold had proceeded so far that the bill, again leaving discretion to the Secretary of the Treasury, could not restore bimetallism. After the closing of the Indian mints matters have become worse, and the solution of the silver question has become still more difficult. What might have been an efficient remedy in 1871 could not have been applied in 1879. What might have been effective in 1879 would have been of no avail in 1890. And if bimetallism is adopted now the method of adoption must be made to fit the circumstances of the day and the possible events of the morrow. No wonder that our greatest statesmen, feeling all this and thoroughly cognizant of the changes that have taken place, cannot to-day advocate measures of which they would have approved twenty years ago, or even five years ago.

What will come next in the history of the battle of the standards? Russia is establishing the gold standard. She certainly does not possess gold enough for this purpose within her own frontiers. She will draw on the gold supply in other countries, and the yellow metal will continue to appreciate. And there are other countries which may adopt the gold standard or may have to increase their proportion of gold. What if England decides to push the coinage of gold in India? What if this country should decide upon a larger reserve for its greenbacks, and if our banks should come to the conclusion that they must keep larger reserves than they now do, and more of gold? While the population increases and the industries of the world naturally would call for an increase in the circulating medium—an increase which cannot possibly be filled by the new production of gold—we have nothing before us but the prospect of a continued appreciation of gold and a continued fall in prices. And at the same time the silver produced will also depreciate. Those who now clamor against what they call the 50 cent dollar would soon raise a cry against what they would call a 40 cent dollar or a 30 cent dollar, and the natural outcome would seem to be the eventual realization or annihilation of the world's legal tender silver money, which in the market for ornaments and purposes of art might possibly bring 5 cents on the dollar.

And how would prices of commodities, real estate, railroad stock, and so forth, then stand? The consequences of the demonetization of silver, serious as they have been hitherto, are really as nothing to what they would be if the principle of demonetization is to be carried out to its full extent. So far we have only stopped further additions to the stock of silver money. We have not yet seriously attempted the more difficult operation of getting rid of what we have.

But let us hope for a brighter future, more sense, and more knowledge. It is more than probable that this great country will find a satisfactory solution, or at least inaugurate a policy that will soon solve the perplexing problem. There is not much faith to be put in the establishment of bimetallism by international agreement, since there cannot very well be any international responsibility for the monetary systems of the world. But as silver has been demonetized gradually, so it will be gradually remonetized by independent action of different nations as soon as they find it to their advantage to follow the example of the country which makes a successful start

MONEY.

In the beginning gold and silver were used as ornaments, gold probably in some localities and silver in others. Vanity prompted man` to shine among his fellow beings, whether it be by a lump of gold to his nose or a silver ring around his finger. All were vain, all wanted the glittering baubles; but the metals were scarce, and only the few and favored could have them. These ornaments became a factor in the dawn of civilization. Instead of killing each other, or robbing each other when famine pressed or the means of sübsistence ran short, men commenced to exchange their ornaments for food. Those who lost their ornaments one season got them back another when they were in affluence and others were needy. Later on the materials, gold and silvor, designated for ornaments, were used more extensively to secure the necessaries of life; and still later these materials were made into pieces uniform in weight and size. That was money. And as the quantity of money increased and only a part of the precious metals were ever used for ornaments, the original purpose for which the metals were intended, was more or less lost sight of. When famine visited Canaan money was sent to Egypt to buy corn. Money had been saved and stored for such an eventuality. And until recent times wise men taught their people to lay up stores of precious metals as being the essence of the wealth of nations.

The fact that money, or originally the material for ornaments, could save a man from starvation, roused human invention and ingenuity. New wants were created and satisfied. The merchant brought the superfluities and peculiarities of foreign countries and exchanged them for money. Factories grew up, commodities were produced and offered by competitors in the market to those who could buy. And those who had money wherewith to buy competed for the commodities offered. Thus prices, or the money value of commodities, were established and clearly depended upon the relation between the quantity of money and the quantity of goods offered. When a man buys he considers in the first place the usefulness, the value in use, to him of the commodity he buys as compared to the usefulness of the money he possesses. In the second place he considers the competing offers from owners of commodities, which owners in making their offers first consider the value in use to them of a certain sum of money as compared to the utility of the goods they possess. Thus the value in exchange, or the price, is determined.

In deciding how much of his stock of money he will spend the buyer will consider not only his actual stock but how soon, or how often, he can replenish it. If he has a certain amount which he is reasonably sure he can replenish regularly in a certain time, say every week, or every two weeks, he is likely to spend or invest nearly the whole of his stock of money in that time. And experience will tell almost everybody in this and other civilized countries that the money he handles is, most of it, turned over in a short space of time. Add to this that credit—I shall recur to this presently—is nothing else than deferred cash payment, and we shall come to two very important conclusions. First, the stock of money in a country is larger than the value of the goods which it turns over in what we may call the period of circulation. Second, there may be a great number of periods of circulation during the long time of a year, and the same money does the same service as many times in the year as there are periods of circulation.

From the above we shall be able to see more clearly the actual relation between money and goods, or how prices are determined, and it is not difficult to understand how sensitive the value of goods must be to the quantity of money at command.

We can also understand that the somewhat prevalent idea that only a small percentage of business is done by money, is erroneous; while it is eminently true that the total stock of money in a country like ours is not worth more than say two or three per cent of the total value of all the commodities turned over in a year, or say only one-fifth of one per cent of the value of the goods turned over in ten years, or the infinitesimal fraction of one-fiftieth part of one per cent of the value of the goods turned over in one hundred years. Prominent defenders of a single gold standard argue that it is of little consequence whether we have much money or little money in the country, because money plays a very small part in the exchange of goods. The argument is false.

RETAIL TRANSACTIONS.

How much money is necessary to transact he business of a working man who earns $2 i day? The per capita circulation would iardly furnish a satisfactory answer, since nany people would use more and many peo- ple would use less money than the working- nan who earns $2. The money is spent with he butcher, the grocer, the dry-goods man, he landlord, and many others. How long a ime does it take for it to circulate through hese hands and then through the bank to eturn to the party who pays the working- nan? Suppose pay-day to be once a week, ind that the $12 then received are spent suc- essively during the week and return to the mployer in that time. Then all the circu- ating medium required by the workingman s $12, and with this amount he transacts his business, which in a year amounts to 52x12, or $624, which is all cash business. I think it far more likely, however, that the circulating period would be two weeks, and the amount of circulating medium required would be $24.

A man who earns $100 a month and is paid once a month, will spend his money gradually during that time, and will need more circulating medium than the man who earns $2 a day.

Those who have still larger incomes no doubt need a still larger circulating medium.

And those who have a very small income will need only a small amount of circulating medium.

How much circulating medium do the people of this country need to transact the retail business of their daily wants? We have about 23 millions of bread-winners who support about 70 millions of souls. If the average circulating medium for each producer were only $10 the total would be $230,000,-

000. This would mean an average circulation per capita of about $3. If the average circulating medium needed by each worker was $30 the total would be $690,000,000; $40 for each would make $920,000,000 and represent about $13 per capita.

Something like this latter amount is probably needed to transact the retail business of this country, which is practically all cash or paid by cash money soon after the debt has been incurred.

For want of statistics it is necessarily difficult to state the amount of the total annual retail trade of the country. But everybody can understand that there is a relation between this annual total, the total of the circulating medium necessary to transact the trade, and the number of the periods of circulation during the year. If the circulating medium is diminished the value of the goods sold is diminished.

Some people are of opinion that only a few per cent of the business of the world is done by actual use of money. This is an error. If the circulating medium is equal to 5 per cent of the amount of the annual business, the number of the periods of circulation during the year must be twenty. The same five dollar bill makes its trade circuit twenty times and pays cash for 100 dollars' worth of goods.

WHOLESALE TRANSACTIONS.

The clearing house exchanges of the country amount to about $60,000,000,000 a year, representing wholesale transactions, transfers of stocks, bonds, real estate, and so forth. This enormous amount is settled between the banks principally by exchanging their customers' checks and drafts, and very little cash money is used in adjusting the comparatively small balances. Strange enough the idea has grown up and become popular that this clearing house business is credit business, not to say actual barter, by which wheat is exchanged for cotton, iron for lumber, stocks for real estate and so forth, and that in all these wholesale transactions money cuts so small a figure that it cannot possibly have any influence on prices. These ideas are wrong. No business can be more strictly cash than the exchanges made by the banks through the clearing houses, for every check and draft is, as a rule, covered by cash money in the banks on which they are drawn. What the clearing house does is not to extend any credits to wheat dealers or iron manufacturers or to facilitate any kind of barter, but simply to save the trouble of counting and transferring the cash money. When the grain dealer draws a check to pay for a cargo of wheat he knows precious little about the doings in the iron and cotton market, but is perfectly acquainted with the cash balance in his bank.

The reserves in the banks furnish the cash money necessary to carry on the wholesale transactions of the country, but the period of circulation in the wholesale business is so short that a comparatively small amount of money will turn over an immense quantity of trade in the course of a year. If the bank reserves in the country amount to $600,000,000 and represent the money necessary for the wholesale transactions of $60,000,000,-000 a year, the period of circulation would be about three days, and the reserves would perform their service of exchanging goods for cash one hundred times in the year.

The banks receive deposits of money and loan out some of it. The amount of reserve kept is principally determined by the probable needs of the depositor, though a minimum reserve may be fixed by law. Generally the banks keep a larger reserve than is actually needed by the customers, and this is particularly the case in times of uncertainty and depression, when idle money is accumulated in the bank vaults. When the banker becomes suspicious of the "times" he cuts down his loans and increases his reserve. Thus money is drawn from the outside or retail circulation, wages and prices fall, less money is needed for the wholesale business, and the actually idle portion of the bank reserves is the only thing that is going up.

Some people think that the volume of

money has nothing to do with prices of commodities, because when prices and wages are falling money is more abundant and "cheap." These people overlook the fact that it is the abundance of idle money in the bank vaults or elsewhere that causes the scarcity of money among the people.

If the bank reserves were thus increased $100,000,000 drawn from the outside or retail circulating medium, what would be the consequence? If the period of circulation had been about eighteen days or one-twentieth part of a year the reduction in wages and incomes, or in prices—if the total quantity of commodities remained the same—would represent $2,000,000,000 a year. In such a case, however, experience has proven that production and trade are reduced, and that, therefore, wages and prices would not fall quite in proportion to the reduction of the circulating medium. Poverty and falling prices usually walk hand in hand in similar cases.

COST OF PRODUCTION AND PRICES.

From time to time it has been asserted that the fall in prices in recent years is to be attributed to a reduction in the cost of production of commodities, and not to the demonetization of silver. The assertion is a fallacy. A reduced cost of production does not lower average prices. Prices represent the value of commodities expressed in money, and as long as the quantities of commodities to be exchanged by a given quantity of money remain the same, the average prices must remain the same, and there can be no exception from the rule. Suppose that one-half of the commodities in the world, hitherto exchanged by one-half of the money, is reduced in cost of production by one-half. The prices could be reduced one-half, and only half as much money as before would be needed to exchange the commodities in question. One-quarter of the world's money could be dropped in the sea, so to say. But it isn't dropped in the sea. It goes to swell the prices of all commodities. Those commodities which are not reduced in cost of production will go up in price, and those commodities which are actually reduced one-half in cost of production will not be reduced one-half in price. The proportion of prices will be regulated according to the proportionate cost of production of commodities, but the average of prices evidently remains the same.

Again, suppose all commodities are all at once reduced one-half in cost of production, or, in other words, that weary mankind in one happy moment discovers how to produce what is now produced in half the time that was formerly needed, is it not simply ridiculous to suppose that prices would be reduced one-half? Everybody ought to be able to see that prices would remain the same as before.

A reduction in the cost of production enables us to produce more commodities, and in order to be able to exchange all commodities at the same average price as before, we need more money. If we are progressive in the arts of production why should we not be equally progressive in the science of money?

COST OF PRODUCTION OF GOLD AND SILVER.

Gold is at present received freely and coined in unlimited quantities at the mints of most countries. When the gold miner starts into business he probably expects to strike a bonanza, but if he does not succeed in this, he is likely to continue mining anyhow, as long as he makes a reasonable profit, and even if he does not succeed in making a reasonable profit the probability is that he will continue until he is broke. He will have to stand certain expenses, but the return for his outlay is most uncertain. Accident plays a great part in the discovery and production of gold, but at the same time there is another circumstance which will partly determine to what extent people will go into the mining business, and that is the value of gold—how much gold can buy. The prices of commodities determined by the stock of money in the world —gold, silver, and paper money—will guide in this respect, and it is natural that when prices are falling, and money is appreciating in value, greater efforts should be made to find gold than when prices are rising and money is depreciating in value. The production of gold and its addition to the stock of money has in itself the tendency to raise prices and in the end to put a limit to the production when prices had gone so high, and the value of gold had fallen so much that it would no longer pay to produce the metal. Thus there is at least a semblance that the output of gold would follow the same law as the output of pig-iron, and be determined in the long run by the cost of production. But when we consider that the stock of money in the world is in round figures $10,000,000,000 —gold, silver, and uncovered paper—and that the annual production of gold is about

$150,000,000, of which probably only $75,000,000 is added to the stock of money, while the other $75,000,000 will be used in the arts, and to make good the wear and tear of the coins in circulation, we find that the increase in the stock of money from this source is only about three-fourths of one per cent—far from enough to fill the increase demanded by a growing population and by what should be a progressive age. The value of our annual gold product simply conforms to the value of the world's stock of money, and it does not matter a particle what it has cost to produce it. If gold rained down from heaven at the limited rate of $150,000,000 a year, and we used it for ornament or added it to our stock of money, what difference would it make? Would its value conform to the value of our stock of money, or would it conform to the cost of production, which in this case would be nothing? Many learned economists, and particularly the defenders of a single gold standard, are so imbued with the cost of production theory that, if a lump of gold worth $150,000,000 was found, so to say, ready made, they would proclaim not only that that lump would have to obey their law of cost of production, and that it would be worth nothing, but that all the gold in all the world must follow the same law as the newly found lump, could not possibly be worth anything, and would have to be demonetized. And if they were inconsistent enough not to say such hard things about gold, they would certainly say it about silver.

What should we say about the white metal and its relation to the law of cost of production? If silver were in the same position as gold, of course it would follow the same rules as gold, and would bear the same relation to the law of cost of production as gold does. But silver is situated differently from what gold is, ever since the demonetization of silver commenced. In some countries we have large stocks of silver in circulation, along with gold, at the ratio of 15 1-2 to 1, and while gold and other money have appreciated considerably in value during the last twenty-three years, this silver money has likewise appreciated in value. In this country we have some $500,000,000 of silver circulating, or represented by circulating paper, at the ratio of 16 to 1, and this silver money is appreciating in value in the same way, along with gold. In India the coinage of silver has been stopped, and while the money in that country consists only of silver, and thus since 1893 is either stationary or decreasing in quantity, it is evident that if there is any progress at all in the way of an increasing production of commodities, the silver money in that country must now be appreciating in value. But in those few countries where silver is still coined without restriction the value of the new production conforms to the value of the money in circulation just as it conforms to the market value for purposes of art. By restrictions in the use of silver for money, by refusing to allow the new silver product by unlimited coinage to conform to the value of the money in the world, the metal has been brought into this peculiar position.—The talk about our "50 cent dollar" is really too absurd, for the very simple reason that we could not throw our $500,000,000 on the market for ornaments, etc., or on the money markets of Mexico or China, and realize anything like 50 cents for 371 1-4 grains. If all countries in the world were to sell their silver money for purposes of art—that is to say, a quantity of some $4,000,000,000, I really do not believe that it would be possible to obtain 5 cents per ounce. Those who have made up their minds that the silver money has to go, might reasonably talk about our silver dollar as our 5 cent dollar or 1 cent dollar. Those who want the silver money to stay, and silver to be rehabilitated, are justified in speaking of our silver dollar as a dollar. Our gold money would be subject to the same laws of value if we treated it in the same way in which we have treated silver. If the world's $4,000,-

000,000 of gold was offered to the goldsmiths to be used for ornaments, the value of it would not be 75 cents an ounce. Everything in this case depends upon the use to which we put our stocks of gold and silver. It would not at all be impossible for this and other countries to decree that the silver dollar should henceforth circulate only as worth 50 cents. Such a measure would please many, who would consider that the right way to bring about an honest silver dollar, which would at last conform to the market price of silver. The only trouble is that such a process would bring with it a contraction of the world's money, and a fall in prices to such an extent that the "market value" of the new 50 cent piece would not be more than about 35 cents.

The idea of the cost of production regulating the value of the stock of silver money is worse than a case of the tail wagging the dog. Suppose the annual production of silver is $100,-000,000, and that of this $50,000,000 were used for money. The money of the world is $10,-

000,000,000. The former amount is the tail, the latter is the dog. Years ago our statesmen got it into their heads that the tail might be wagging the dog, and so they cut it off. Now they have discovered that the loose tail is wagging the dog.

In connection with the above, I would make a remark about the mine owners' profit. A good many people object to the rehabilitation of silver on the ground that it would add enormously to the wealth of the owners of silver mines. These people, in the narrowness of their views, would sacrifice the happiness of mankind for the pleasure of spiting a few successful mine owners. As a matter of fact, we have thousands of silver mines in this country alone, and the vast majority of them have yielded little or nothing, while the cost of working them has been very great. In short, some very good authorities have estimated that on an average more than two dollars is expended for every dollar's worth of silver brought out of the ground. Silver mining is a speculation, in which the profit naturally accrues to the few successful ones. If all the silver mining was to be done, say, on government account, it would very soon be found that the cost of production was too large to allow any silver mining at all.

DO WE NEED MORE MONEY?

Prices have fallen enormously ever since the demonetization of silver commenced. During the last quarter of a century trade has been depressed, though there have been a couple of revivals, between 1880 and 1882, and between 1890 and 1892. The old rule of a business crisis occurring every ten years seems to have been reversed, and instead of it we have now more or less of a continual. crisis, with little bits of revivals now and then. One of the causes of this state of things is certainly the insufficiency of money, bringing about the fall in prices. Nor can it be long before it is generally recognized that a continued fall in prices must be a powerful obstacle in the way of progress and enterprise. Individuals now rarely enter into any industrial undertaking on their own risk, unless they can pay for the whole plant, for experience has taught them that a plant which to-day costs $100,000 will in five years not be worth $75,000, and that ten years hence it will be worth still less. If you were to build a factory for $100,000, and in doing so had to give a mortgage for $50,000, your property would be out of your hands after a certain time, unless the profits had enabled you to pay off the mortgage. For this reason industrial undertakings are more and more coming into the hands of corporations, and the prospects for the individual are becoming slimmer, and the ultimate result is that the industrial organizers become more cautious, and the number of unemployed grows larger.

To what extent are our great railroad systems affected by falling prices? Freight rates must be reduced like the price of any other commodity, and the income drops. The operating expenses may be reduced in proportion, but the interest on the bonds remains the same, and eventually the road goes into the hands of a receiver. The worst consequence, however, is that railroad construction is discouraged, no new fields are opened up, and it has even been proposed in Illinois that the state government should undertake the responsibility of deciding whether a proposed new railroad would be needed or not, before granting a charter—this for the purpose of protecting the earnings of the old roads. The trouble is, there is no incentive to progress; there is stagnation, there is less employment, and there is less provision for the growing population—and all this because there is not enough money.

The farmers probably suffer more than any other class of our citizens, except those who suffer by not being able to get any work. In this country a very large number of farmers have mortgaged their farms, some for the purpose of improving them, others because they could not pay the whole of the purchase money when they bought. The falling prices of farm produce have reduced the money value of that part of the produce which would otherwise have satisfied the mortgage holder. The mortgage will weigh heavier and heavier on the farmer, and in thousands of cases every year the farm is lost. The farmer becomes a renter, there is less inducement to till the soil, and for many the chances to become tramps are greater than ever.

All these things produce uncertainty and lack of confidence among traders and others who from time to time speculate on the demand for goods and give orders to manufacturers or wholesale dealers. Business is curtailed, production is cut down, work is scarce, and enforced idleness is plentiful. But if the country at large and the masses are losers, there are a few who gain by falling prices. Bond and mortgage holders and creditors in general are best off, and apparently gain what others lose. Falling prices are, indeed, a most powerful element in making the rich richer and the poor poorer.

A stock of money sufficiently large to maintain a steady average of prices or an average fluctuating as little as possible would evidently be conducive to greater prosperity, and a more just distribution of the good things in this world. For the sake of justice and progress we need more money.

The latter half of the nineteenth century will go to history as divided into two distinct and widely different periods. The first commences with the gold discoveries in California and Australia, and culminates in 1873. It is marked by large accessions of gold to the world's stock of money—"giving wings to trade"—by rising prices, by wonderful progress, by unwonted enterprise and prosperity, by railroad building, and constantly increasing manufacturing. It was an era which promised every young man a future, and encouraged him to action. Yet to that period belong the greatest wars in the history of the world, and the contracting of the largest national debts. But these calamities could not stem the onward tide.

The second period is marked by demonetizations of silver, resumptions of specie payments, introductions of the gold standard, contractions of the world's stock of money—pinioning the wings of trade—falling prices, stagnation, absence of enterprise, and lack of employment. It is an era of little promise for the future. Yet we live in profound peace, and national debts have been reduced. But these blessings cannot stem the downward current.

There is one kind of contraction to which I would draw especial attention. Elsewhere I have pointed out the reasons for temporary fluctuations in the amount of money held by the banks as reserves, and the money in circulation among the people—the one falling as the other rises, and vice versa. The same law evidently obtains on a larger scale in regard to long periods of progress as against long periods of depression and increasing uncertainty. Let us compare the present standing of the three largest European banks to what it was fifteen years ago, or about the time this country had completed its resumption process:

	Dec. 1880. Millions.	Mch. 1896. Millions.
Bank of France—		
Gold	$105	$390
Silver	245	250
Bank of England—		
Issue department	200	315
Bank of Germany—		
Coin and bullion	135	235
Total	$685	$1,190

This table shows in those three banks alone an increased holding of gold of about $500,000,000. At the same time the uncovered note issue of the Bank of France and the Bank of Germany is now $75,000,000 smaller than it was in 1880. In all, this is nearly $600,000,000, and for the most part represents a contraction which is counteracted to but a very small degree, if any, by any new supply of gold, which latter has been needed, probably to its full extent, for resumptions or the adoption of the gold standard in various countries, or may be has not even been sufficient for such purposes. Nor need we flatter ourselves that the habits of the people have changed so considerably in favor of notes instead of gold. The fact is, that the banks in general holding large reserves prefer to have some of it in notes, and for this reason the large increase in the note issues of the banks in question simply indicates a still larger increase in the bank reserves throughout those countries, and a corresponding contraction. As regards the banking department of the Bank of England, the reserve which fifteen years ago was satisfactory at thirty or thirty-five per cent, is now kept up to seventy per cent.

The chain of cause and effect is this: When silver was demonetized, or the coinage of it stopped, the stock of silver money in the banks became more or less "unavailable." The gold reserves had to be increased. The scramble for the yellow metal commenced. Contraction and uncertainty of trade followed. Traders and merchants who could do it, protected themselves by more ready cash, and this again caused increase in bank reserves. At present the Bank of France alone has an "unavailable" stock of silver of $250,-000,000, and on top of that it has an available stock of gold of $390,000,000. When bimetallism is restored, but not until then, can a change be expected. When the stocks of silver money in the world are made "available" trade will be easy, the money reserves will be reduced, the circulation will be larger, prices will be steady, or may even rise, and prosperity will be at hand.

While European banks have been increasing their stock of gold, and Russia has been storing up gold in anticipation of resumption, the government of the United States has made no change in its provision for the gold reserve behind its greenbacks. While the Bank of France has a note issue of about $725,000,000, backed by $250,000,000 of silver and $390,000,000 of gold, or together $640,000,000—or, as some would make the comparison, deducting $250,000,000 covered by silver, $475,000,000 of notes covered by $390,000,000 of gold, or about 82 per cent—we have $346,000,000 of greenbacks covered by only $100,000,000 of gold, or about 29 per cent. If we had followed the same policy as Europe, by contracting our money and raising our gold reserve to 80 or 100 per cent, it is reasonable to suppose that there would have been no outward drain on the treasury.

BIMETALLISM.

Bimetallism is the union of two kinds of monometallism. How such a union at any time was brought about can easily be understood. One country had a single silver standard, the adjoining country had a single gold standard. Along the border line between the two countries commodities sold on one side of the line for a certain quantity of silver, on the other side for a certain quantity of gold. If the relative value of gold and silver, or the ratio between the metals, happened to be fairly steady, what could be more natural than that the people along the border should be indifferent to which metal they used as money at the ratio established by custom? And what would be the consequence of such indiscriminate use of either metal at the ratio established by custom?

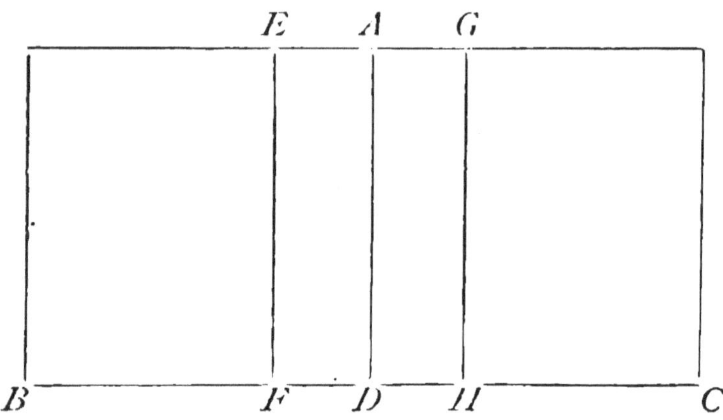

In the above diagram AB represents the gold country, AC the silver country, and AD is the frontier line. EH is the territory where either metal is acceptable, or where the demand for gold or silver is elastic. If the production of gold predominates, gold will flow into territory AH, and drive some silver into GC. If silver becomes predominant, the flow will be in the opposite direction. And all the time the same ratio is maintained, that is to say, as long as the bimetallic territory is large enough to create a sufficiently elastic demand for either metal.

Originally bimetallism established itself,

or was established by the voluntary or unconscious use of either metal at a customary ratio, and later on it was confirmed by people declaring through their government that either metal at the customary ratio should be acceptable to or used by all citizens, or should be a legal tender in payment of debts, public taxes, and dues.

If a ratio can thus be maintained by the elastic use of the respective metals, it is evident that the ratio can be changed by limiting the use of one metal and extending the use of the other.

Bimetallism has been thoroughly tested in practice, and has been found to work to perfection. Such was the case in France, where it was in operation between 1803 and 1873 at the ratio of 15 1-2 to 1. During the whole of that period the value of the gold and silver coins in France never deviated in the slightest degree from the established ratio. At the same time London was the chief market place for silver, and from there we have the quotations for silver bullion, which naturally varied somewhat, according as silver was flowing to or from France.

According to the adopted ratio the value of silver coins was 60.84 pence per ounce, at the same time the charge for coining was 0.45 pence per ounce; the average interest while bullion was coined may be set down at 0.15 pence per ounce, and, in case the exchanges were such that gold went to England while silver went to France, this charge would be equal to 0.60 pence per ounce. In all, these charges would amount to 1.20 pence, and if this amount is deducted from the value of the coin, 60.84 pence, the minimum price of the bullion in London would be 59.64 pence. Now, if we look up the statistics of the price of silver we shall find that until silver was demonetized by Germany, the price of silver bullion in London never went below 59 7-8 pence, and this happened once, in the spring of 1852.

After Germany had discarded silver the mint of France was so pressed that it took a considerable time to coin the bullion that was sent in, and in one case, just before the mint was closed, the Rothschilds were notified that they would have to wait a year for the coinage of bullion to be sent in by them. The interest may be placed in this case at, say, 4 per cent per annum, and would amount to 2.28 pence per ounce, which would reduce the price of silver bullion in London to the figure 57.36 pence, and that was just about the price that silver commanded in 1874, just before the closing of the French mint.

Now, on the other hand, suppose that gold was flowing into France, and silver was exported, say over London or Southampton to India, how would the case stand then? The price of silver in France, that is, of the silver coins, according to the adopted ratio, was 60.84 pence per ounce. The exchanges were such sometimes that the cost in bringing the silver to London would be equivalent to about

1 per cent, or say, 0.61 pence per ounce, which, of course, would to that extent enhance the value of silver bullion in London. At the same time there was another item that should be taken into account, and that is the abrasion of the coins. In the "History of Prices," by Tooke, we find that the abrasion was so great as to cause a loss of 3 per cent to the exporter. Now, suppose that this item would only represent a loss of 2 per cent when a large number of coins were bought, this would involve a further charge of 1.22 pence per ounce, to that extent further increasing the value of bullion in London. Now, these three items would make the price of bullion in London 62.67 pence per ounce, and we find that in July, 1859, the price of silver bullion in London reached the figure of 62 3-4 pence per ounce. In that year France exported over England to India the enormous sum of $75,000,000.

From the above we can easily understand that if France had charged no seigniorage, if she had always kept her silver coins up to full weight, and if she had issued silver certificates of small denominations instead of keeping depositors of bullion waiting for their coins, silver bullion in London could never have varied in price more than would have been occasioned by the fluctuation in the rate of exchange between London and Paris.

WHAT WOULD HAPPEN IF IN THIS COUNTRY WE ADOPTED UNLIMITED COINAGE OF SILVER AND GOLD AT THE RATIO OF 16 TO 1?

When we have come to the conclusion that more money is wanted in this country, and we attempt to devise plans for satisfying the want, we must bear in mind, in the first place, that many other countries have similar kinds of money to what we have, and that, therefore, the money of the world is, to some extent, so to say, common property, of which each country has its share, and not more than its share, distributed, and from time to time redistributed, according to certain economic laws. If this country was to add to its money a larger quantity than would be called for by the increase in population, and the expected increase in the volume of business—for the purpose of maintaining steady prices—the surplus would belong, so to say, to the world, and some of our money would flow out. For this reason it would be a mistake to think that we could retain the stock of money we have and add to it any quantity we please.

If free and unlimited coinage of silver and gold at the ratio of 16 to 1 is adopted, the first question will be: "What would be, say, the annual addition to our stock of money?" When, under the Sherman act, we bought for coinage 4,500,000 ounces of silver a month, the price of the new silver product was raised considerably, yet not to a point corresponding with the ratio of 16 to 1, which is $1.29. If all silver that can be produced at the latter price is accepted at the mint a stimulus would be given to silver mining and, in all probability, the annual addition to our silver money would run up to a figure of from $60,000,000 to $70,000,000. We should also have to receive a small contribution from the stock of silver money in Mexico, from where silver would flow until the money of that country was at par with the money of this country. From eastern countries, like China and India, there would not be the slightest danger of any silver flood, because the period of circulation of money in those countries is exceedingly long; their commerce is small, and their money is used chiefly for hoarding—to be brought out in times of famine and distress. Nor is it fair to suppose that the great European nations would make this country a dumping ground for their silver, because, in the first place, the sentiment in favor of bimetallism in those countries is sufficiently strong to prevent such a policy, and, in the second place, those countries could not stand the ruinous result which would inevitably follow the tremendous appreciation of gold, and fall in prices that would be called forth by such a policy.

If silver was remonetized in this country we could thus calculate on a yearly addition to our money of something like $75,000,000 in silver, but as this amount would also be an addition to the world's stock of money we should have to share with the world, and should lose part of our gold. If we command about fifteen per cent of the world's money, our net gain would probably be some $12,000,000 a year, that is to say, we would gain about $75,000,000 silver and lose $63,000,000 gold, which latter would go to Europe and other parts of the world, besides what gold we may have to furnish from our mines, as we might suppose, on first consideration. Such an outflow of gold would not, however, occur. Paradoxical as it would seem the current would at first and for some time be in the opposite direction. Gold would actually come from Europe to this country. And the reason for this is very simple. As soon as we have restored bimetallism the value of silver is restored. This would make the silver in Europe "available;" the scramble for gold would cease; the bank reserves would diminish; more money would get into circulation, and some of it would come to us. Such would be the effect in Europe where one country after another would soon follow our example.

Some really terrible prophecies have been made as to the immediate future, if we adopt the unlimited coinage of silver at 16 to 1. Here are some of them:

1. The instantaneous disappearance from circulation of all our gold, which would at once be hoarded.

2. Our silver dollar would be worth only 50 cents.

3. The wages of the workingman would be worth only one-half of what they are worth now.

4. Commodities would double in price.

5. National repudiation and dishonor.

Now, any man with one grain of common sense ought to understand that if gold disappeared, and if silver—and, of course, our paper money also—fell to one-half its present value, there would be a contraction of our stock of money from $1,500,000,000 to less than $500,000,000, and prices and wages would fall in one lick about 67 per cent. Surely the foreigner would come here with all the gold needed to restore prices. Such, at least, has been the rule as long as false prophets have existed. Wouldn't the fellow who had hoarded his gold be glad to buy wheat for 20 cents a bushel and sell it for export for 60 cents and make 200 per cent profit, and thus let out his treasure into circulation? Wouldn't he do his country that favor for an extra profit of only 100 per cent, or 50 per cent, or 25 per cent, or 5 per cent—all extra? Or, may be, out of pure patriotism, he would do it just for the ordinary profit. There is nothing like appealing to people's feelings. And, as for the poor bondholder, why, he would get as many dollars as before, only now he can buy for that money three times as much wheat as he could before, and he can sell it for three times as much money as he paid, by exporting it, and thus realize 15 per cent where he only got 5 before the national repudiation. Wouldn't he do something towards whitewashing our national dishonor, and restoring the old order of things?

Verily, it is tiresome to have to refute such a lot of balderdash.

To be sure, an attempt may be made, and, no doubt, it will be made, to corner gold, but the only effect it can have will be to turn the exchanges in our favor, or bring gold here, if the circulation is appreciably affected. If the stock of gold in course of time becomes very low, and the country be practically on a silver basis, there may certainly be some manipulation of gold in fixing from day to day the exchanges with gold countries. If we restore unlimited coinage at the ratio of 16 to 1 we may in about ten years be on a silver basis, particularly if Europe persists in its present monetary policy. But much may happen in ten years to prevent such an occurrence, and if France alone, in the course of a few years, would fall into line with the United States, the bimetallic territory would probably be more than sufficiently large to maintain permanently the ratio of 16 to 1, or 15 1-2 to 1.

CONCLUSION.

We have seen what would be likely to happen if we adopt unlimited coinage of silver and gold at the ratio of 16 to 1:

1. Gold would at first and for some time come to us from Europe by the reduction of the European bank reserves.

2. Other countries would follow our example in restoring bimetallism, and the silver question would be solved for good.

But in the extremely improbable event of no other country following our example for some time to come, we are still strong enough, or our country is large enough, to maintain bimetallism, or to keep both metals in circulation. For, in the first place, as we add silver to our circulation we may gradually add gold to our greenback reserve to the extent of $246,000,000 beyond what is at present prescribed by law. And, in the second place, such a seigniorage might be charged as to practically control the amount of silver offered for coinage. I might say something as to the disposition of such seigniorage, but after the ratio of 16 to 1 has once been adopted I hardly think we shall have any occasion to charge a seigniorage.

Science and experience have amply proven the usefulness of bimetallism. Justice and the needs of the people demand its restoration.

www.ingramcontent.com/pod-product-compliance
Lightning Source LLC
Chambersburg PA
CBHW030717110426
42739CB00030B/705

* 9 7 8 3 7 4 3 3 2 0 6 2 8 *